MVP BOOKS

AVAILABLE NOW
from Lerner Publishing Services!

The *On the Hardwood* series:

ON THE HARDWOOD

GOLDEN STATE WARRIORS

ZACH WYNER

On the Hardwood: Golden State Warriors

MVP Books
2255 Calle Clara
La Jolla, CA 92037

MVP Books is an imprint of Scobre Educational, a division of Book Buddy Digital Media, Inc.,
42982 Osgood Road, Fremont, CA 94539

MVP Books publications may be purchased for
educational, business, or sales promotional use.

Cover and layout design by Jana Ramsay
Copyedited by Susan Sylvia
Photos by Getty Images

ISBN: 978-1-61570-914-4 (Library Binding)
ISBN: 978-1-61570-913-7 (Soft Cover)

TABLE OF CONTENTS

Chapter 1
FROM PHILLY, WITH LOVE

In California's Bay Area—a region that includes San Francisco, Berkeley and Oakland—basketball is as much a part of the social landscape as Haight Street, Alcatraz Island, People's Park, or the Golden Gate Bridge. From high school gymnasiums, to Oakland's famous Mosswood Park (where NBA greats Gary Payton and Jason Kidd grew up playing) to Oracle Arena, home of the Golden State Warriors, basketball is ever-present and ever adored.

In many ways, the history of basketball in the Bay Area mimics the history of the land and its people. The history of the Bay Area is one of struggle and perseverance, of

resistance and triumph. The anti-war movement, the free-speech movement, the Occupy Wall Street movement, and the movement for Gay Rights all flourished in the Bay Area because of a combination of exceptional leaders and a collective love for humanity. A similar recipe of

The Golden Gate Bridge links San Francisco and Marin County and is the most photographed bridge in the world.

Paul Arizin poses for an action shot during the 1950 season.

exceptional players and a collective love for the game breathed life into the sport of basketball. In 2013, the Golden State Warriors captivated basketball fans in the Bay Area and beyond with a magical playoff run, but this franchise announced its greatness to the world long ago.

Originally from Philadelphia, Pennsylvania, the Warriors were the first-ever team to be crowned NBA champions. In 1947, they defeated the Chicago Stags four games to one and captured the BAA Title. (BAA was changed to NBA after the league merged with the NBL in 1949.) Nine years after their first title, Hall of Famers Paul Arizin, Michael Bryson, and Neil Johnston led the Philadelphia Warriors to another championship, becoming the second NBA team to own multiple titles. Still, perhaps the biggest moment in the early history of the franchise came in 1959, when they signed Wilt "The Stilt" Chamberlain.

Wilt "The Stilt"—a 7'1", 275-pound behemoth—was an athlete the likes of which the NBA (and possibly the world) had not yet seen. Combining great size, strength, agility and grace, Wilt broke every scoring record in existence and forever changed the way basketball was played.

In 1962, the Philadelphia Warriors moved west to the Golden Gate City and became the San Francisco Warriors. The city could not have asked for a better team. Coming off a season in which they had come up just short against Bill Russell's Boston Celtics, the Warriors seemed destined to be a force for years to come. In 1961-62, the Warriors final season in Philadelphia, Wilt Chamberlain averaged 50.4 points and 25.7 rebounds per game, setting a scoring mark that may never be broken. In addition to the averages, Wilt scored 100 points in a single game against the New York Knicks. Wilt Chamberlain's arrival in the Bay Area signaled good times on the horizon. As long as Wilt was a Warrior, the Warriors would be at the top of the league.

In the 1963-64 season, the San Francisco Warriors became the kings of the Western Conference. Led by Chamberlain's 37 points and 22

Chamberlain and Bill Russell battle for a rebound.

Board Kings

rebounds per game, the Warriors marched through the playoffs and faced the Boston Celtics in the NBA Finals. While this was a first for Bay Area fans, this was not the Warriors' first rodeo. As the Philadelphia Warriors, they had done battle with the Celtics before. They knew that no matter how well they'd played to get there, the task that stood before them was the tallest. After losing the first two games of the series, the Warriors destroyed the Celtics in Game 3, 115-91. But when Boston eked out a narrow, three-point victory in San Francisco in Game 4, the Celtics squashed the newly kindled hopes of Warriors fans. Boston hung on to win a close Game 5 and their fans celebrated the Celtics' sixth straight title. Meanwhile, Warriors fans put aside their disappointment and focused on their team's bright future.

Chamberlain posts up Russell and looks for the entry pass.

However, that bright future didn't pan out exactly as people had hoped. By the middle of the next season, the Warriors were at the bottom of the Western Conference with an abysmal record of 11 wins and 33 losses. Noting the growth of back-up center Nate Thurmond, Warriors owner Frank Mieuli traded Wilt to the Philadelphia 76ers.

Wilt was sad to leave the Bay Area. The 1960s in America were difficult times and Philadelphia was a city full of racial tensions. The Civil Rights Movement was in full swing, and the rights of African Americans were beginning to be recognized; however, Philadelphia lagged behind San Francisco in its acceptance of racial equality. When asked about his departure from the

Wilt shoots a jumper over Bill Russell.

west coast, Wilt said, "I had fallen in love with San Francisco, and I was rather sad to leave." Fans were rather sad too. Happily, both Wilt and the Warriors would find themselves enjoying better times in the not-so-distant future.

Big Man, Big Legacy
Wilt is one of only five players in NBA history to win four or more MVP awards.

If there was ever a team that had an excuse to stop believing in their ability to win, it was the 1965-66 San Francisco Warriors. The 1964-65 team went 11-33 with Wilt Chamberlain, and they won only six games after he left. Luckily for the Warriors, the NBA tries to create a silver lining for every losing team. In today's NBA, this silver lining is the chance to participate in the Draft Lottery and nab a college basketball standout. In 1965, things were even simpler: the two teams that finished in last place were awarded the first four picks. Having finished at the bottom of the Western Conference, the San Francisco Warriors got the first two picks of the draft.

Rick Barry entered the 1965 NBA Draft having just led all of college basketball in scoring. At the University of Miami, a school better known for its football than its basketball program, the 6'7" forward scored 37.4 points per game during his senior season. In Rick Barry, the Warriors found a player who could score and make his teammates better. One of those teammates was the young Warriors' center who had

Rick Barry stands on the court prior to a game.

been Wilt's back-up, a rebounding machine who would one day be regarded as one of the NBA's 50 Greatest Players.

In 1965, Nate Thurmond was on the verge of greatness. An eventual seven-time All-Star and five-time NBA All-Defensive first or second teamer, Nate provided toughness, defensive intensity, and the kind of rebounding that just does not exist in today's NBA. Also known as Nate "The Great," Nate Thurmond is still the team's all-time leader in rebounds (12,771), and minutes played (30,729). But the numbers don't begin to describe Nate "the Great's" importance to the Warriors franchise. As the team's current Warriors Legend and Ambassador, Nate "the Great" is in the stands for every Warriors home game. To this day, fans stop to say hi and introduce their kids to the center of the Bay Area's love affair with the Warriors. Thurman, along with Rick Barry, led the Warriors back to the top of the sport.

Nate Thurmond.

1967 was the Summer of Love in San Francisco. Hundreds of thousands of people were migrating to the Haight-Ashbury district to be a part of a hippie culture that celebrated love and peace. The success of the San Francisco Warriors fit right into the groove. By the end of the 1966-67 regular season, the Warriors were back in the playoffs as the West's top seed. Rick Barry led the league in scoring with 35.6 points per game and Nate "the Great" averaged 18.7 points and 21.3 rebounds. Even people that had not previously taken an interest in sports embraced Rick Barry, Nate "the Great," and the rest

Nate "the Great's" size, strength, and aggressive play intimidated centers throughout the league.

of the Warriors team.

The Warriors rode those good vibes all the way to the NBA Finals. Waiting for them was former teammate Wilt Chamberlain and a 76ers squad that had just become the first team to beat the Boston Celtics in the playoffs in eight years. But this didn't scare San Francisco. Barry averaged 40.8 points per game in the series and the Warriors beat the Sixers twice. The 76ers eventually won the series in six games, but the people of San Francisco and Warriors owner Franklin Mieuli were hopeful for the future. They had two of the game's biggest stars just entering the prime of their careers. Or so they thought.

After the 1966-67 season, in a move that shocked the basketball world, Rick Barry left the Warriors and signed with the Oakland Oaks of the ABA (American Basketball Association). When asked about his decision Barry said, "This is the way I support my family... If everything was based just on loyalty, no one would ever make any money." The comments were a harsh reminder that professional basketball is a business. For fans, the notion that the players might have a different set of concerns than they do was hard to accept. Many thought Barry would

Al Attles attempts a shot during the 1967 NBA Finals.

Hall of Fame center Bob Lanier attempts to guard Nate the Great in the post.

forever be a villain to the Warriors franchise.

While the Warriors were undergoing a painful break-up with their star forward, the team's relationship to San Francisco was also changing. Games at The Cow Palace in Daly City (located just south of San Francisco) were not all that well attended, and players and fans alike complained about the smell. Named "Cow Palace" because it hosted rodeos and livestock events, it was not the ideal arena for a basketball team. Before the 1971-72 season, the team permanently relocated to Oakland and changed their name to the Golden State Warriors.

The city of Oakland had long been a hub of the basketball world,

Going Home... Again?
In 2012, the Warriors announced their intention to move the team back to San Francisco in the coming years.

Civil Rights leader Dr. Martin Luther King, Jr. was assassinated in the spring of 1968.

presidential candidate Robert Kennedy were assassinated in one horrifying two-month span. Across the country, Americans were showing their frustration with their country's wars, overt racism, and disregard for the poor. And in Oakland, a deadly exchange between police officers and Black Panther founder, Huey Newton, symbolized the struggle between law enforcement and oppressed minorities. The city was too preoccupied with social and political affairs to give much thought to the new basketball team. After two seasons of poorly attended games, including the 1968-69 ABA Championship, the Oaks moved to Washington D.C.

but in 1968 and 1969, its people had not shown any interest in Rick Barry's Oakland Oaks. The United States was enduring difficult times. The country was fighting an unpopular war in Vietnam, and at home, civil rights leader Martin Luther King, Jr. and

Oakland Activists

While attending Merritt College in Oakland, Huey Newton and Bobby Seale organized the Black Panther Party in 1966.

Barry spent three seasons playing back east, but by the 1971-72 ABA season, he was longing to return home. The Golden State Warriors were a talented team, getting far more attention than the Oakland Oaks had a few years before. In a moment of refreshing humility, Barry and the Warriors put aside their differences and agreed on a deal. During a forgettable four-year span in the ABA, Barry had been traded twice and sustained multiple knee injuries. Now he was returning to the very team that he said he would never play for again. But his teammates and the city of Oakland welcomed him back, and the Warriors quietly grew into something no one saw

coming: NBA champions.

For two years, the city of Oakland cheered the dynamic duo of Rick Barry and Nate "the Great" as they led the Warriors to winning records. But before the 1974-75 season, Warriors ownership determined that the team needed an infusion of youth. They traded Nate "the Great" to the Chicago Bulls for Clifford Ray,

Nate "the Great" battles Bucks star, Kareem Abdul-Jabbar, for rebounding position.

a young 6'9" center who was coming off his best year as a pro. In addition to this move, the Warriors had drafted UCLA star Jamaal Wilkes, and University of San Francisco All-American, Phil Smith. The team was younger, faster, and built to score. Pouring in 108.5 points per game, the 1974-75 Warriors scored more than any other team in the league.

Rookie of the Year Jamaal Wilkes drives past Bullets star Elvin Hayes.

The Warriors rode Rick Barry's 30.6 points and 6.2 assists all the way to the Western Conference Finals where, as fate would have it, they encountered the Chicago Bulls and their former teammate Nate "the Great." With a trip to the NBA Finals on the line, the Warriors rallied for a huge Game 6 win in Chicago and then barely edged the Bulls in the deciding Game 7 at home, 83-79. Despite the victory, they entered the NBA Finals as huge underdogs to Elvin Hayes, Wes Unseld, and the mighty Washington Bullets.

NBA analysts were not the only ones surprised by the Warriors run to the finals. Having expected them to be eliminated by late spring, the Oakland

Coliseum had already scheduled other events on the days that the finals were supposed to take place. With no alternative, the Warriors shrugged their shoulders and crossed the Bay Bridge, returning to their old digs at the Cow Palace. But if their pride was at all injured, the Warriors didn't show it. Instead they went out and beat the Washington Bullets in four straight games. The Warriors overcame deficits of 14 points in Games 1 and 4, and 13 points in Game 3, to pull off the historic sweep.

When asked about winning the championship, Finals MVP Rick Barry said, "It has to be the greatest upset in the history of the NBA Finals. It was like a fairy-tale season. Everything just fell

Historic Barrier Falls

The 1975 NBA Finals was the first championship game or series in pro football, baseball, hockey, or basketball to feature two African American head coaches—Al Attles and K.C. Jones.

into place. It's something I'll treasure for the rest of my life." He was not alone in treasuring the moment. Elated Bay Area basketball fans joined him in celebrating Northern California's first NBA crown.

Rick Barry battles Wes Unseld for the rebound.

Chapter 3
NELLIE BALL

The run of great basketball in the Bay Area didn't end in the 1975 NBA Finals. For the next two seasons Barry, Wilkes, Smith, and the Warriors were factors in the playoffs. Unfortunately the trio never again played for a championship. After a 1978-79 season in which the Warriors failed to make the playoffs for the first time in four years, Rick Barry left California to finish his career in Houston. After his departure, the Warriors suffered through a nine-year nightmare in which they failed to make the playoffs. Funny that a man nicknamed "Sleepy" would be the one to wake them up.

In the 1987 playoffs, the Warriors won their first playoff series in 10 years against the Utah Jazz before

Eric "Sleepy" Floyd scored a playoff-record 29 points in the 4th quarter against the L.A. Lakers.

meeting the "Showtime" Los Angeles Lakers in the Western Conference Semifinals. Trailing Magic Johnson's team 3-0, Warriors guard Eric "Sleepy" Floyd erupted in Game 4 for 51 points (a record-setting 39 coming in the 2nd half) and the Warriors beat the Lakers, 129-121. It wasn't a trip to the finals, but it was a step in the right direction. With the hiring of a new coach in 1988, the Warriors looked to follow that winning path.

Coaches are characterized in many different ways. There is the consistency coach like Gregg Popovich, whose team plays great defense and finishes at or near the top of their division every year. There is the player's coach like Doc Rivers, who forms tight bonds with his players and gets the most out of his team. There is the disciplinary coach like Pat Riley, who rides his players hard and lets them know when they are not meeting his expectations. Then there is the wild-card coach like Don Nelson, the kind of coach who breaks every basketball convention and is willing to take large risks in order to maximize his team's potential.

For many years Don Nelson brought "Nellie Ball"—a fast-paced, offense-oriented style of play that sometimes worked and sometimes didn't—to the Golden State Warriors. Whatever your opinions of Nelson and Nellie Ball, there's no denying his importance to the Golden State franchise and the positive impact

Tim Hardaway drives the lane for an acrobatic lay-up.

he had on players like Chris Mullin, Tim Hardaway, Mitch Richmond, Stephen Jackson and Baron Davis. Nellie's "Run TMC" team of the late 1980s (the TMC standing for stars Tim, Mitch, and Chris), and the "We Believe" Warriors of 2006 through 2008, played a style of basketball that energized a fan base and got the attention of the entire country.

Don Nelson's first contribution to the Warriors franchise was in 1988 and had little to do with basketball. For three seasons, former All-American, Chris Mullin, had been failing to meet expectations. When the Warriors had selected him with the #7 pick in the 1985 Draft, they believed they were drafting a sure thing. But

3,000 miles from his hometown of Brooklyn, New York, a lonely and homesick Chris Mullin struggled with personal issues. When Don Nelson arrived as an assistant coach in 1987, he recognized that Mullin needed help and encouraged him

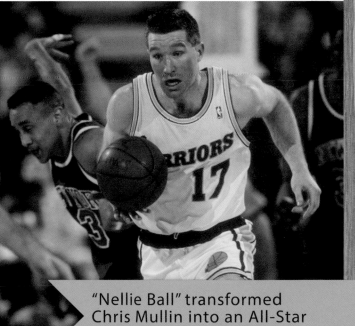

"Nellie Ball" transformed Chris Mullin into an All-Star and a Dream Teamer.

to leave basketball for a while and seek treatment. Mullin entered a rehabilitation clinic, missed 22 games, and emerged 48 days later a changed man.

In the 1988-89 season, a leaner, meaner Chris Mullin averaged a career best 26.5 points per game. The Warriors made the playoffs and swept the 2nd seeded Utah Jazz. They fell in the second round, but Mullin's emergence as one of the league's top scorers, as well as a big-game player (he averaged 29.4 per game in the playoffs), stoked Warriors fans' hopes for the future. And the future was electric. In 1988, Mullin teamed up with Kansas State University star Mitch Richmond, and in 1989, rookie Tim Hardaway joined the party. The incendiary trio was known as "Run TMC."

The 1989-90 Warriors didn't make the playoffs. They didn't even finish the season with a winning record. At 37-45, the casual fan might not have thought that there was much to talk about. But if that fan watched the way this team competed, if they witnessed the joy the Warriors took in scoring a league-leading 116 points per game, they would have

Mitch Richmond jukes a defender and turns the corner.

seen what the excitement was all about.

This excitement spilled over into the 1990-91 season, a season in which there was no threesome in the league that could match the numbers put up by the Warriors trio of Chris Mullin (25.7 points per game), Mitch Richmond (23.9 points per game), and Tim Hardaway (22.9 points and 9.7 assists per game). In fact, Run TMC was so good at scoring the basketball that coach Don Nelson would often tell them to forget the playbook. According to Chris Mullin, "On a given night, Nellie would give us the freedom to just go out there and play. He'd say, 'tonight, I'm going to call no plays. As long as you guys are sharing the basketball, playing

Tim Hardaway keeps his head up and looks for an open teammate as he pushes the ball up the court.

the right way… no plays.'"

Who needed plays when you had the Warriors pushing the ball up the court on every possession? Who needed plays when you had point guard Tim Hardaway breaking opponent's ankles on every drive to the basket? Hardaway's signature

Name That Trio
The name "Run TMC" was chosen by the players after The *San Francisco Examiner* sponsored a "Name the Warriors Trio" contest.

Breaking Up Is Hard To Do

Mitch Richmond was traded to the Sacramento Kings for Billy Owens, a promising 6'9" forward whom the Warriors believed would bring them the size they needed to advance in the playoffs.

move, the crossover dribble, created all kinds of opportunities for his sharp-shooting teammates. Don Nelson put his faith in Tim Hardaway to lead his offense and Hardaway rewarded him by leading the Warriors to three straight wins over the San Antonio Spurs and a first-round playoff series victory.

Sadly, Run TMC only lasted two seasons. Before the 1991-92 season, Mitch Richmond was traded to the Sacramento Kings and the excitement generated by the highest scoring trio in the league fizzled. A few years later, Tim Hardaway was traded to the Miami Heat and the dismantling of Run TMC was complete. In many ways, the rise and fall of this team reflected American greed of the 1980s and 1990s. Instead of appreciating their good fortune and building around the players that brought them success, the Warriors wanted more. Trades made in an effort to get bigger, faster, and better damaged team chemistry. In the years that

Mitch Richmond was a six-time All-Star as a member of the Sacramento Kings.

28

followed the break-up of Run TMC, fans watched their beloved Warriors sink into a funk from which it seemed they might never recover.

In 2004, two-time Olympic Gold Medalist and future Hall of Famer, Chris Mullin, was hired as Executive Vice President of Basketball Operations. Two years later, Don Nelson returned from an eight-year stint in Dallas to coach the Warriors.

Timeless Appeal

After more than 20 years, Run TMC T-shirts are still available online and numerous highlight reels can be viewed on YouTube.

Nelson and Mullin were reunited to breathe life into a team that had not made the playoffs in 10 years. Nelson knew exactly how he was going to do it: let the reins loose on point guard Baron Davis and bring Nellie Ball back to Golden State.

An excited Warriors squad gathers during a timeout.

When Baron Davis came to the Bay Area, he became the first superstar to don a Warriors uniform since Chris Mullin left for Indiana nearly a decade before. By 2006, management had built a team around Davis that included Stephen Jackson, Jason Richardson, Al Harrington, and the young scoring-machine drafted straight out of high school, Monta Ellis. Engineered to run, these Warriors caught fire in the last months of the 2006-07 regular season, winning 16 of the last 21 games. They stormed into a memorable playoff series against the #1 seed Dallas Mavericks.

Having lost in heartbreaking fashion to the Miami Heat in the 2006 NBA Finals, the Dallas Mavericks and superstar Dirk Nowitzki were desperate for another shot at the title. That said, no one could overlook the fact that the Warriors and their up-tempo style posed the Mavericks some problems. Having beaten Dallas in all three regular-season match-ups, the Warriors were a confident bunch. They came into the series with some serious swagger, and in Game 1 they backed

The Dallas Mavericks simply could not stay in front of speedy point guard Baron Davis.

Baron Davis acknowledges the ecstatic Oracle Arena crowd following a Game 6 win.

There is no way to measure a crowd's impact on a game. No statistic expresses a crowd's ability to fluster the opposing team or uplift their own players. But no one can possibly deny the 2007 Oracle Arena crowd's influence on the Warriors/ Mavericks series. Those fans created a home-court advantage the likes of which basketball has rarely seen. With the motto "We Believe" stamped in blue lettering across their gold shirts, these Warriors fans were the loudest and most raucous crowd in recent memory. The players heard them, and they responded by making history.

The 2006-07 Warriors won Games 3 and 4 in Oakland and then routed the Mavericks in Game 6, 111-86, to advance Golden State

that swagger up, beating Dallas, 97-85, on their home floor. Dallas came back to tie the series at one game apiece, but in Games 3 and 4, the Mavericks got a dose of something they were unaccustomed to: an energized Oracle Arena.

Superstar Numbers

In the 2006-07 playoffs, Davis dominated, averaging 25 points, seven assists, five rebounds a three steals per game.

to the second round of the playoffs for the first time since Run TMC had beaten the Spurs back in 1991. Starting the second half of play in Game 6, the Warriors held a slim two-point advantage, but a 24-3 run in the third quarter keyed by four Stephen Jackson three-pointers put the game away. It was the first time in the history of the NBA that a #8 seed had beaten a #1 seed in a seven-game series. And while the Warriors eventually lost to the Utah Jazz in round two, the thrill of winning basketball reverberated in the Bay Area for the entire offseason.

Dubious Distinction

The Mavericks joined the 1994 SuperSonics, the 1999 Heat, and the 2012 Bulls as the only #1 seeds to lose to a #8 seed.

Warriors forward Mikael Pietrus tries to dunk over Andrei Kirilenko during the 2007 Western Conference Semifinals.

Throughout the 2007-08 season, Warriors fans came out in droves. Indeed, 32 of 41 home games were sold out. Baron Davis and Monta Ellis—arguably the most explosive backcourt in basketball—led the team to a 48-34 record, their best since 1994. Unfortunately, the Western Conference was loaded. For the first time since the league had expanded the playoffs to 16 teams, a team with 48 wins did not qualify for a playoff spot. The "We Believe" era came to an abrupt end.

Following the disappointment of being the best team ever to not make the playoffs, Baron Davis signed with the Los Angeles Clippers, and a fan base unprepared to suffer another letdown mourned the loss of their star. The next four years were marred by injuries, and Warriors fans sadly watched as their team fell from contention.

In 2007-08, Davis and Ellis were arguably the most explosive backcourt in the league.

In 2010, the country was once again in bad shape. Two years into a painful recession, the Bay Area was again at the center of a political movement. The Occupy Oakland protests dominated local news as the city's inhabitants rallied behind workers, immigrants, the unemployed, and the veterans of American wars fought in Afghanistan and Iraq. The protests called attention to the issue of tax dollars being used to bail out big banks while ordinary people struggling to pay their mortgages and feed their families were overlooked and ignored. Once again, professional basketball seemed less important than the social and economic challenges facing the people. And with the Warriors finishing the 2010-11 season 10 games under .500 anyway, there didn't seem to be much to cheer about.

In the shortened 2011-12 season, the Warriors won only 23 games under new coach Mark Jackson. If this was a preview

of what was to come, it looked like more tough times for the Golden State. But appearances were only skin deep. Something special was brewing in Oakland, something that no one but those closest to the team could sense.

Coach Mark Jackson convinced his young players that they could compete with the league's best.

Steph Curry grimaces in pain after injuring his ankle in a game against the Dallas Mavericks.

record was understandable. Before the 2011-12 season began, team owners and players were unable to agree on how to divide the money generated by the league and there had been a lockout. With the teams locked out of their facilities, there was a shortened training camp and preseason. As a result, Coach Jackson did not have enough time to teach his system to the players. The lockout finally ended and a shortened, 66-game schedule was drawn up, but with little time to prepare for the season, NBA players began dropping like flies. The injury bug hit the Warriors hard. Among others, Stephen Curry, the promising point guard whom many hoped

Before the start of the 2011-12 season, Mark Jackson had guaranteed the Warriors would make the playoffs. That prediction looked foolish when the team finished the season with 23 wins and 43 losses. But upon closer examination, their poor

Impressive Debut

In the 2011-12 season, rookie Klay Thompson scored nearly 13 points per game and was named to the NBA's All-Rookie First Team.

would grow into a star that year, battled ankle injuries and played in only 26 games.

The 2012-13 season was a different story. With training camp and a full preseason under their belt, these Warriors knew who they were and what they expected of themselves. And it didn't take long for the rest of the league to realize that these expectations were higher than Warriors teams of recent years. Back in the mid-1990s, a culture of losing infected the Warriors like an illness. In 2007, they seemed to change that culture, to rejoice in their good health. But that good health hadn't lasted; the sickness had returned. In 2012-13, the Warriors not only got well, they stomped that sickness to smithereens. In addition,

Steph Curry celebrates after draining a three-pointer.

they energized a fan base that had forgotten what it was like to root for a winner, a fan base that had forgotten the strength and energy that can be gained from cheering on a team that demonstrates the values at the heart of every successful movement.

Chapter 5

WE ARE WARRIORS

Stephen Curry was a great shooter coming out of high school, but he was also undersized. Despite his basketball lineage (his father Dell Curry played in the NBA for 16 seasons), at six feet and 160 pounds, not a single major-conference university offered him a scholarship. Curry attended Davidson College and spent the next three years giving headaches to all those coaches who had recruited lesser players. In fact, in his sophomore year at Davidson, Curry led his 10th-seeded Wildcats all the way to the Elite 8 in the NCAA tournament. On the way he set a tournament record by scoring over 30 points in his first four NCAA tournament games. The guard with the sweet jump shot who had been overlooked by every major university in the nation was looking like an NBA lottery pick. Following his junior season, he declared himself eligible for the NBA Draft. For the Golden State Warriors—as had been the case when they drafted

Steph Curry is embraced by a teammate after an upset victory over Georgetown University.

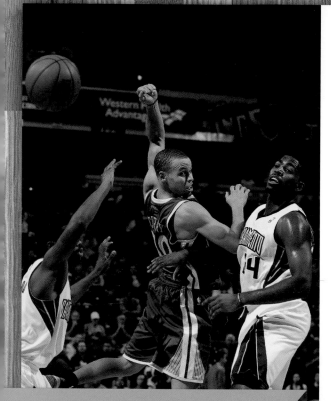

Steph attempts a tricky over-the-shoulder pass during a visit to Sacramento.

competition every night will expose your weaknesses. Unless a team has extraordinary talent, remarkable endurance and a tremendous work ethic, it will fade in the standings. For the 2012-13 Warriors to bring their fans back to basketball, they needed more than a strong start. The belief that this team was for real came when the Warriors went 12-4 during the month of December—a stretch that included a 6-1 road trip.

Teams that lack mental toughness don't go 6-1 on the road. The rigors of travel, of not sleeping in your own bed, of long flights and hours spent shuffling around airports, and eating on the go take their toll. Teams that go 6-1 on a seven-game road trip must have toughness, discipline, and a number

Chris Mullin—seven was their lucky number.

In the NBA, teams can over-achieve for a while, but sooner or later the challenge of facing NBA-level of different players that can step up and take over a game. Finally, they must possess a trait that none of the highly entertaining teams from the Nellie-ball era could boast—they must play solid defense.

The 2012-13 Warriors squad could score from every position on the floor. Power forward and co-captain David Lee, acquired from the Knicks back in 2010, averaged 18.5 points and 11.2 rebounds per game. Lee's consistency helped him become the first Warrior selected to play in the NBA All-Star game since 1997. Steph Curry upped his scoring average to 22.9 (including 26 per game after the All-Star break), and Harrison Barnes, the 6'8" rookie out

David Lee soars for a breakaway dunk.

of the University of North Carolina, utilized a combination of grace and explosiveness to become one of the great young prospects in the league. Meanwhile, shooting guard Klay

Lucky #7
Harrison Barnes, Stephen Curry, and Chris Mullin were all drafted seventh in the NBA Draft.

Klay Thompson shoots over Joe Johnson during a road game in Brooklyn.

basketball heritage. His father, Mychal Thompson, was the #1 overall pick in the 1978 NBA Draft, and in 1987 and 1988, he helped the Lakers win consecutive NBA titles. Much like Klay, Mychal helped his team by playing strong defense. Unlike Klay, the bulk of his scoring was done close to the basket. In the 2012-13 season alone, Klay made 211 three-pointers—210 more than his dad made in his entire career.

Thompson, in only his second year in the league, averaged 16.6 points per game while shooting 40% from three-point range.

Like Stephen Curry, Klay is another Warrior with impressive

Stephen Curry, Klay Thompson, Harrison Barnes, and David Lee all made outstanding contributions to the Warriors season, but their contributions only told part of the story. Chemistry and depth made the Warriors consistent winners during the 2012-13 season. That

Son of a Champ

Klay's father, Mychal, was the 1st pick in the 1978 NBA Draft and was a two-time NBA champion.

Andrew Bogut boxes out Tim Duncan during a playoff game against the Spurs.

depth came in the form of Jarrett Jack, Carl Landry, rookie Draymond Green, and the former #1 draft pick that had been at the heart of the Monta Ellis trade, Andrew Bogut. Coming off a foot injury, the seven-foot-tall Bogut played in only 32 games, but he averaged nearly eight rebounds and two blocks in 25 minutes of playing time. The 28-year old Australian-born center gave the Warriors a presence in the middle of the floor that they had not had since Nate Thurmond left town for Chicago in 1974. Come playoff time, that presence helped take Golden State to another level.

Entering the playoffs against the 57-win Denver Nuggets team, Mark Jackson made some noise about his two starting guards' place in history. "I've watched the history of the game as player, as a fan, as an announcer, as a young kid, and

Shooting Stars

Curry and Thompson were one of only 11 backcourts in NBA history in which both guards averaged more than two three-pointers per game.

I've not ever seen two guys in the same backcourt shoot as well as these two guys," Jackson said. The numbers backed up his statement. No backcourt in the history of the league had taken or made as many three-pointers as Thompson and Curry, and they did it shooting a combined 43% (the fourth best percentage of all time). They are also only the 2nd pair of teammates ever to hit 200+ throws. Take into account the fact that these guys created many of their own shots, and there's no denying the significance of their achievement. Curry and Thompson are not merely spot-up shooters who run off a series of screens and receive a pass. Many of their shots are taken off the dribble. While Jackson's comments may have sounded like exaggeration, his analysis was spot on. The 2012-13 Warriors backcourt was historic and deserves recognition. In the first round of the 2013 playoffs, their historic shooting ability made

Curry approaches the free throw line where he is a career 90% shooter.

headlines nationwide.

The Golden State Warriors' 2013 playoff run lasted 12 games. They won six and lost six, eventually getting knocked out by an experienced San Antonio Spurs squad led by Tony Parker and Tim Duncan. But the story of this playoff run was not one of wins and losses. It was about the way the Warriors competed. It was about the level of skill and desire they demonstrated. It was about their ability to win in a hostile environment. And it was about the way their players and fans fed off of one another, electrifying a city that had fallen upon some hard times and needed something to cheer for.

Curry shoots an acrobatic runner over Tony Parker.

The 2013 playoffs were filled with too many big moments to count. Twice, Steph Curry scored 22 points in a quarter, draining threes from seemingly impossible angles and driving to the hoop for finger-

Klay soars past Danny Green for the two-handed slam.

rolls lofted over the outstretched fingertips of seven-footers. Klay Thompson scored 29 in the first half of Game 2 in San Antonio, hitting eight of nine three-pointers and reminding Warriors faithful of "Sleepy" Floyd's 39-point half back in 1987.

It seemed that every time this young Warriors team fell behind, veteran leader Jarret Jack would hit two or three jump shots and then Carl Landry would take a hard foul, make the shot, flex his biceps and go to the free throw line to complete the three-point play. All-Star David Lee, lost in the first game of the playoffs to a torn hip flexor, miraculously came off the bench to play in the Spurs series. The injured Lee added some big-time buckets and contributed selflessly to the cause. Andrew Bogut averaged 10 points, two blocks, and 14 rebounds, giving the Warriors the promise of a balanced inside-outside attack for years to come. And rookie Harrison Barnes grew up before the nation's eyes, nearly doubling his season averages by scoring 16 points and grabbing six rebounds per game.

Apparently, the bigger the moment and the better the competition, the better Harrison Barnes plays.

The Bay Area's identity is wrapped up in politics. Its social and political movements are a source of pride. Many Americans move to the Bay Area to be a part of that culture. Some mistakenly believe that sports and politics don't mix—that people who have a love for one cannot have a love for the other. Nothing

could be further from the truth. Communities that root together, grow together. And few causes unite and energize the Bay Area like the Golden State Warriors. The Warriors give people with different values and different backgrounds common ground on which to stand. In an

Harrison Barnes shoots over the outstretched arm of Manu Ginobli.

ever-changing world, what could be more valuable?

In a world sometimes short on joy, Steph Curry, Klay Thompson, Harrison Barnes, and Andrew Bogut play the game like a group of kids who haven't a care in the world. That kind of joy is as rare as it is infectious. It is cause for celebration. It is the reason 20,000 screaming fans refused to leave Oracle Arena after their team was eliminated and instead chanted, "Warriors! Warriors!" It is the reason those fans will be packing Oracle Arena in the future, supporting their squad, instilling in them the belief that they are the group that will lead this team back to the pinnacle of their sport—the NBA Finals.

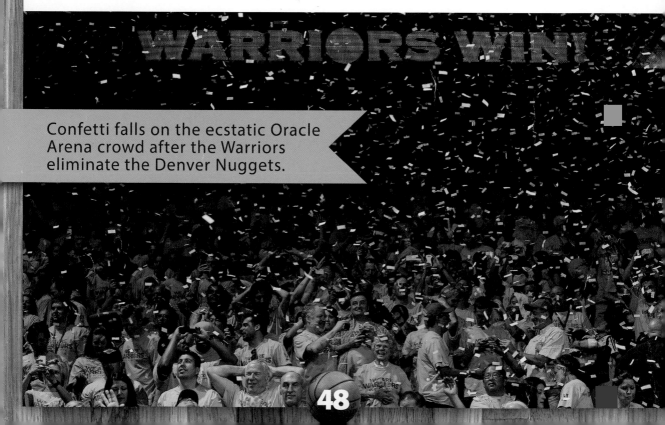

Confetti falls on the ecstatic Oracle Arena crowd after the Warriors eliminate the Denver Nuggets.

48